Religious Freedom in America: The Background and Importance of the Religious Freedom Restoration Act of 1993 on Current Affairs and Religious Liberty

Matthew A. Brown

Table of Contents

Introduction 5

Balancing Religious Freedom with Rule of Law...........................9

Congress's Response – The Religious Freedom Restoration Act13

The RFRA and Current Events 17

Conclusion 21

About the Author 23

Other Books by Matthew A. Brown 25

Annotated Bibliography...27

Notes 31

Introduction

There are two things you do not discuss in public. You do not discuss religion; you do not discuss politics, and you definitely do not discuss them together. Both of these areas tend to be very divisive issues in today's society. They can easily take any cordial conversation and turn it into a full-fledged shouting match very quickly. This is unfortunate because these are two of the issues that mean the most to history, culture, and the future.

Religion is very prominent throughout history. It has been the guiding force for kingdoms and empires. It has been the leading cause of wars and also of peace. For hundreds of years during the Middle Ages, religion was the main factor that determined almost everything that went on in the world. Religion has played a major role in the formation of the current culture.

The other major factor that has determined how people live is politics. Many people think "politics" is a dirty word that they associate with a bunch of egotistic men in a dark back room making shady deals to get more money in their own pockets. While this has been the case at times, it is thankfully the exception more than it is the rule. Politics is the art of compromise. Politicians negotiate in order to find a solution that would make the country better. Politics has had as much if not more of an effect on today's culture and society as religion has. It affects the economy, the way of life, and the societal norms. Politics shape the direction of a country and consequently shapes the culture and the way of life for its citizens.

The United States is unique because it was one of the first countries to be created upon the concept of a republic where the people chose representatives to be their voice in government. It was also founded on the principles of freedom. One of the main freedoms is the freedom of religion, and one of the laws that is currently dictating how one looks at the freedom of religion is the Religious Freedom Restoration Act of 1993, also known as the RFRA.

In this book, societal norms will be broken and both religion and politics will be the topics of the conversation. The background of religious freedom in the United States including the first settlers, the Virginia Statute for Religious Freedom, and the First Amendment will be discussed. The Supreme Court case *Employment Division v. Smith (1990)* that sparked the writing of the RFRA will be dissected, and the debate and discussion that Congress conducted when writing the RFRA as well as the text of the bill will be dug through. The application of the RFRA will be looked at in *City of Boerne v. Flores (1997)* and in the controversial decision that was handed down earlier this year in *Burwell v. Hobby Lobby Stores, Inc. (2014)* and how the RFRA and the *Hobby Lobby* decision will be important moving forward. The paper will end with a discussion of the RFRA's role in future legislation and case law. All of these topics will point to the fact that the United States has placed a high value on religious freedom and that the Religious Freedom Restoration Act of 1993 has been one of the ways the country has worked hard to protect that freedom.

The United States of America has had a long history of religious freedom. Some of the first settlers came to the New World in search of a place to worship without the intrusion of government. The Pilgrims were one of the first of these groups. They fled England because they did not agree with the teaching of the Anglican Church, the official church of England. In America, they found a place where they could worship freely, and since then, people throughout the colonies and later the United States enjoyed that same freedom.

One of the first codifications of the Freedom of Religion was by Thomas Jefferson in the Virginia Statute for Establishing Religious Freedom, also referred to as the Virginia Statute for Religious Freedom. The statute was originally drafted in 1777 but was not first introduced into the Virginia General Assembly until 1779 where it died in the legislative process. It was not until 1786 when statute was reintroduced by James Madison into the Virginia General Assembly that it was actually passed and signed into law on January 19, 1786. The statute is considered the predecessor to the First Amendment and to the Supreme Court's understanding of the Freedom of Religion.[1]

The Virginia Statute for Religious Freedom declares that a person cannot be discriminated against because of their religious beliefs. They also cannot be forced into or hindered from religious practices. Jefferson asserts that the right to the Freedom of Religion is a natural right given by God. God made the mind free. To coerce the mind into believing and practicing something that it does not believe only leads to hypocrisy and does not nurture the development of thought and knowledge which Jefferson believes are essential to a free society. If a person is allowed to believe as they wish, and debate and discussion are encouraged; then truth will abound. False teaching will not stand the scrutiny of debate and will not be tolerated by a society that searches for the truth. People do not have the right to dictate what others can or cannot believe and practice. They have no authority over what God created as free.[2]

Jefferson's Statute was later incorporated into the First Amendment. James Madison led the effort to get the Freedom of Religion added to the Bill of Rights. Even though he did not believe the rights listed in these new amendments needed to be enumerated, Madison realized that the new Constitution would not be ratified if they were not added, and he championed for the Freedom of Religion to be included. Much debate occurred as to the wording of the free exercise and establishment clauses. The framers wanted to make sure that they embodied the relationship between church and state correctly. They came up with the Establishment Clause which states that Congress shall make no law respecting the establishment of religion and the Free Exercise Clause which states that Congress shall make no law prohibiting the free exercise of religion. These two clauses based on Jefferson's Statute and other colonial constitutions and laws have provided the structure for government policy on religion up until recent history.

Balancing Religious Freedom with Rule of Law

All of this background and precedent was overlooked in 1990 in the Supreme Court case *Employment Division, Department of Human Resources of Oregon v. Smith*, 494 U.S. 872 (1990). In this case, two men, Alfred Smith and Galen Black, were fired from their job as drug rehabilitation counselors at a private rehabilitation center after they took the hallucinogenic drug peyote during a religious ceremony for the Native American Church. When they applied for unemployment assistance, they were denied by the State of Oregon because their dismissal was due to "work-related 'misconduct.'"[3] The State Court of Appeals reversed the decision on the basis that Smith and Black's First Amendment rights for the free exercise of religion were violated. The decision was affirmed by the United States Supreme Court on remand on the condition that the use of peyote was not in violation of the State of Oregon's controlled substance law. Later, the Oregon Supreme Court concluded that the use of peyote for sacramental uses was in violation of the controlled substance law but ruled that in this case, the law infringed on Smith and Black's free exercise rights and was invalid. In short, the Oregon Supreme Court ruled that the controlled substance law was invalid when it infringed on a person's free exercise rights of the First Amendment.[4]

For a review of the second Oregon Supreme Court decision, the case went to the United States Supreme Court and was argued on November 6, 1989. The decision was handed down on April 17, 1990. Justice Antonin Scalia wrote the opinion of the Court for himself, Chief Justice Rehnquist and Justices White, Stevens, and Kennedy. Justice O'Connor wrote a concurring opinion which Justices Brennan, Marshall, and Blackmun joined without concurring. Justice Blackmun wrote the dissent for himself and Justices Brennan and Marshall. The

Court reversed the previous ruling and held that the state is permitted under the Free Exercise Clause to prohibit the use of controlled substances even when the use is for religious reasons.[5] The Court's reasoning was that the state had the authority to forbid or require an act that is part of a religious duty as long as the law is not directed at the religious act. The case cited for this line of reasoning is *Reynolds v. United States*, 98 U.S. 145 (1879), which handled the matter of whether or not polygamy would be allowed if a person's religious beliefs required them to practice it. *Reynolds* holds that a law that inadvertently violates a person's religious practices is constitutional as long as it is constitutional when it is applied to a nonreligious situation. Justice Scalia, in the opinion for *Employment Division v. Smith*, quotes the opinion of the Court in *Reynolds*:

Laws are made for the government of actions, and while they cannot interfere with mere religious belief and opinions, they may with practices...Can a man excuse his practices to the contrary because of his religious belief? To permit this would be to make the professed doctrines of religious belief superior to the law of the land, and in effect to permit every citizen to become a law unto himself.[6]

Scalia cites that the only time that a religiously neutral law may be waived on account of a religious practice is when the Free Exercise Clause that protects the free exercise of religion is combined with another protection in the Constitution such as freedom of press or freedom of speech such as in, among those cited in the opinion, *Cantwell v. Connecticut,* 310 U.S. 296 (1940), *Murdock v. Pennsylvania,* 319 U.S. 105 (1943), *Follett v. McCormick,* 321 U.S. 573 (1944), and *Wisconsin v. Yoder,* 406 U.S. 205 (1972). According to Scalia, *Employment Division v. Smith* does not combine two protections as these cases did and therefore does not warrant the Court to hold that "when otherwise prohibitable conduct is accompanied by religious convictions, not only the convictions but the conduct itself must be free from governmental regulation"[7] as was requested by the respondents. The Court ordered that Oregon may deny the respondents unemployment compensation because they were fired for conduct that was prohibited under Oregon law. The prohibition was constitutional, and the denial of compensation was consistent with the Free Exercise Clause of the First Amendment.[8]

Justice O'Connor agreed with the holding of the Court based on the question it was presented, but not the reasoning by which the Court reached its decision. She believed that to broadly say that if the exercise of religion is incidentally prohibited by a regulation that is applied generally and validly then the First Amendment has not been encroached upon, is a false interpretation of the First Amendment and the Free Exercise Clause. She does not believe the opposite either. To allow a person to ignore a law based solely on the fact that it was against their religious beliefs is dangerous. Citing previous First Amendment jurisprudence in *Cantwell* and *Reynolds*, Justice O'Connor wrote, "We have recognized that the freedom to act, unlike the freedom to believe, cannot be absolute."[9] Justice O'Connor believes that the Court should be following the rule set in *Sherbert v. Verner*, 374 U.S. 398 (1963). The Sherbert Test balances the First Amendment Free Exercise Clause with the government's interest in regulation by forcing the government to justify any infringement on a person's free exercise of religion and that infringement must be as minimal as possible.[10]

In the Supreme Court's dissent, Justice Blackmun did not see anything wrong with the ceremonial use of peyote. He agreed with Justice O'Connor that the Sherbert Test should be the test that is used to determine the validity in Free Exercise cases rather than the ruling of the Court in *Employment Division* which makes the free exercise of religion a "luxury"[11] that cannot be available in a regulated country. He also stated that in this case the state did not present enough evidence that its interests outweighed those of the petitioners. The state did not attempt to enforce the restriction against peyote. The ceremonial use of peyote did not impede the state's war on drugs or further drug trafficking in the state. On these grounds, the state did not have the authority to infringe on the petitioners free exercise rights.

The *Employment Division* decision departed from the popular Sherbert Test for determining validity in free exercise claims. The Sherbert Test said that, in order for law that infringed on the free exercise of religion to be valid, the government had to demonstrate a compelling interest and the infringement had to be in the least restrictive means possible. *Employment Division* departed from that test and said that the free exercise of an individual alone could not make a law invalid. It had to be combined with another interest.

Congress's Response – The Religious Freedom Restoration Act

In response to the drastic change in free exercise jurisprudence, Congress was whipped into action. Numerous bills were introduced to restore the Sherbert Test as the method of determining the validity of free exercise claims. The first major bill on this subject was S. 2969 introduced in the 102nd Congress by Senator Edward "Ted" Kennedy (D-NY) on July 2, 1992.[12] Senator Kennedy reintroduced the bill as S. 578 into the 103rd Congress on March 11, 1993 with sixty cosponsors.[13] Another major bill restoring the free exercise of religion was H.R. 1308, introduced in the House of Representatives by Representative Charles "Chuck" Schumer (D-NY) on March 11, 1993 with 107 cosponsors. [14] All of these bills were very similar in nature. They all wanted to reverse the ruling and new precedent of the Supreme Court in *Employment Division v. Smith*. In a US Senate Committee on the Judiciary hearing on S. 2969 on Friday, September 18, 1992, Senator Kennedy, Chairman of the Committee, made the following comment in his opening remarks:

The brave pioneers who founded America came here in large part to escape religious tyranny and to practice their faiths free from government interference. The persecution they had suffered in the old world convinced them of the need to assure for all Americans for all time the right to practice their religion unencumbered by the yoke of religious tyranny.[15]

Senator Kennedy then described the protections that the Founders placed in the Bill of Rights to protect the Freedom of Religion: "That profound principle is embodied in the two great religion clauses of the first amendment, which provides that Congress 'shall make no law respecting the establishment of religion or prohibiting the free exercise thereof.'"[16]

Religious Freedom in America

Senator Kennedy wanted to stress the importance of the history and background and the original wording of the Constitution to fellow lawmakers, judges, and government officials as well as to the public. During floor debate on S. 578 on the Senate floor on October 26, 1993, Senator Kennedy quoted a concurring opinion of Justice Souter in *Church of Lukumi Babalu Aye, Inc. v. Hialeah*, 508 U.S. 577 (1993), another case involving the Free Exercise Clause and the decision in *Employment Division v. Smith*, "Neutral, generally applicable laws are drafted as they are from the perspective of the nonadherent have the unavoidable potential of putting the believer to a choice between God and government."[17] Senator Kennedy and the other senators who co-sponsored S. 578 did not want to force the public to have to make that decision between God and government because they knew what the Bible says in Acts 5:29b, "We ought to obey God rather than men,"[18] and that the governmental interest would lose to the religious practice many times in the minds of the public. These senators wanted to create a statute that gave greater lenience to the religious communities in the country by allowing their interest to be weighed against the government's interest.

The bill that ended up being passed was Representative Schumer's bill, H.R. 1308. It passed the House of Representatives by a voice vote on May 11, 1993. After a slight amendment changing a couple of words, H.R. 1308 was passed by the Senate on a vote of 97-3 on October 27, 1993, in lieu of S. 578. The three nay votes were from Senator Byrd (D-WV), Senator Helms (R-NC), and Senator Matthews (D-TN). The House passed the Senate's amended version without objection, and President Clinton signed the Religious Freedom Restoration Act of 1993 into law on November 16, 1993 making it Public Law No: 103-141.[19]

The nation now had a statute declaring that the United States or any state government cannot substantially burden an individual's religious exercise without providing that the burden is a result of a compelling government interest and is the least burdensome method of fulfilling that interest. The statute also provides that it does not alter the First Amendment's Free Exercise or Establishment Clauses.[20]

The Religious Freedom Restoration Act was the law that applied to all Free Exercise cases at the federal and state level until 1997. In the Supreme Court case *City of Boerne v. Flores*, 521 U.S. 507 (1997), the Archbishop of San Antonio, Patrick Fernandez Flores, requested a building permit to expand the church in Boerne, TX, because the congregation had outgrown the building. The City of Boerne denied the permit because the church was a contributing building in a zoned historical district and to alter the building would be to compromise the historical integrity of the building and the district. The Archbishop sued the city citing the RFRA claiming the denial of the permit was an infringement on his and his congregation's free exercise rights as they could no longer all worship in the building without adding more space. The District Court ruled that the RFRA should not apply to state issues because Congress overreached the enforcement power it was given in § 5 of the Fourteenth Amendment. The Fifth Circuit heard the case on appeal and reversed the decision of the District Court. The United States Supreme Court granted certiorari.[21]

Congress based its authority to pass the Religious Freedom Restoration Act and to enforce the Free Exercise Clause of the First Amendment at the state level on the Fourteenth Amendment. The Fourteenth Amendment guarantees that the state cannot, without due process, deprive a citizen of life, liberty, and property. Section five of the Fourteenth Amendment states that Congress has the authority to enforce this with "appropriate legislation."[22] The question before the Supreme Court in *City of Boerne v. Flores* was whether the RFRA is an appropriate piece of legislation based on § 5 of the Fourteenth Amendment. The Court denied the archbishops claim that the RFRA was an appropriate enforcement of § 5 of the Fourteenth Amendment because that section authorizes laws that are either "preventive" or "remedial."[23] While it is difficult to determine the line whether a law fits into this category or not, the Court determined that the RFRA did not. It also claimed that the distinctness of federalism was not observed when the RFRA was applied to the states. It created an unnecessary overreach of the federal government onto state matters that § 5 of the Fourteenth Amendment did not intend to allow. Based on these principles, the Supreme Court struck down the Religious Freedom Restoration Act as it applied to the states.[24] The RFRA's application at the federal level was not in question in this case and remained intact. The question of whether the RFRA applied to federal cases was later upheld in the case *Gonzales v. O Centro Espirita Beneficenteuniao Do Vegetal*, 546 U.S. ___ (2006).[25]

The RFRA and Current Events

The current event surrounding the Religious Freedom Restoration Act is the Supreme Court case *Burwell v. Hobby Lobby Stores, Inc.* 573 U.S. ___ (2014). This is the case that raised the question of whether an employer could opt out of providing certain contraceptives under the Patient Protection and Affordable Care Act (ACA) that the employer deemed to be against their religious beliefs. The Supreme Court had to decide whether the Religious Freedom Restoration Act applied to a for-profit corporation as well as whether the government's interest in supplying healthcare outweighed the religious conviction against supplying these certain forms of contraception.

Many groups were interested in this case. Churches and religious organizations lobbied to protect their religious rights. Women's Rights and Feminist groups viewed the case as a women's choice issue. Universal healthcare supporters did not want a ruling that would hurt or discredit the already controversial Affordable Care Act. This case had a large impact for a lot of people.

Hobby Lobby Stores, Inc. and Conestoga Wood Specialties Corporation sued Sylvia Matthews Burwell, Director of United States Department of Health and Human Services (HHS), for an exemption of the contraception mandate of the Affordable Care Act. The request for an exemption was denied by the district court. The Tenth Circuit Court reversed the decision and ordered HHS to stop enforcement of the contraceptive mandate on Hobby Lobby. In other similar cases, two circuit courts agreed with the Tenth Circuit while two other circuits came to the opposite decision. The decision was appealed to the U.S. Supreme Court which granted certiorari.

Religious Freedom in America

The Supreme Court found that closely held corporations such as Hobby Lobby, Conestoga, and Mardel qualified for the free exercise protections in the Religious Freedom Restoration Act. Health and Human Services argued that Hobby Lobby, Conestoga, and the other corporations involved in the case did not fall under the free exercise protections provided by the Religious Freedom Restoration Act because they were for-profit corporations and not "persons." The Court had previously found that non-profit corporations do fall under the RFRA's provisions in the case *Gonzales v. O Centro Espirita Beneficenteuniao Do Vegetal*, 546 U.S. ___ (2006). HHS failed to make a substantial argument as to why a for-profit corporation should not be considered a person as it is under the Dictionary Act, 1 U. S. C. § 1. There is no reasonable definition of a "person" that included individuals and non-profit corporations, without also including for-profit corporations.[26]

HHS also argued that corporations could not exercise religion. The Court also found this to be an unsatisfactory argument. As previously stated, the Court already decided that non-profit corporations qualified for the RFRA protection in *Gonzales*. There is no reason why for-profit corporations cannot exercise religion under the same recognition as non-profits especially since the court, in a separate case, has already recognized the free exercise rights of merchants who were trying to make a profit. The Court finds that business practices that are designed to make a profit are protected under the free exercise clause and consequently the RFRA.[27]

The Court also found that the corporation's free exercise of religion was substantially burdened by the contraception mandate that HHS put out as a part of the Affordable Care Act. The owners have a firmly held religious belief against providing contraceptives that work after conception believing they work to abort the unborn child. HHS burdened this religious belief by mandating that the health coverage the employer must provide must include these contraceptives and assigning a penalty of at least $2,000 per employee per year if the minimum requirements for health coverage under the ACA are not met. This created a severe economic burden on the corporations.[28]

Lastly, the Court found that while providing cost-efficient health care to the nation was a compelling government interest, the mandate by HHS to provide these contraceptives was not the least restrictive means of attaining that goal. The Court mentioned other ways that HHS could provide these methods of contraception without burdening employers' free exercise of religion through the mandate. These included the government paying the cost of these contraceptives or HHS providing the same exemption that they give to religious groups and non-profits to closely held for-profit corporations. The Court was also very clear in stating that this decision was only applicable to the contraception mandate and could not be applied to other areas or be thought of as a broad decision that allowed anyone to be exempted from any part of the ACA mandates because of a loosely held religious belief.[29]

The *Hobby Lobby* decision proves that the Religious Freedom Restoration Act will be a key piece of legislation in the upcoming years. As the Affordable Care Act continues to go into effect, more and more issues will need to be addressed some of which might possibly be religious. The decision of the court that closely held for-profit corporations are considered individuals is very closely related to the *Citizens United* case which said that corporations are treated as individuals for campaign finance purposes. If legislation were passed to alter the definition of person or individual in response to *Citizens United*, it could have a major effect on the contraception mandate and the *Hobby Lobby* decision. There have been cases across the country where bakers, photographers, and other service providers were sued because they refused to provide their services to homosexual wedding ceremonies. Although *City of Boerne* declared the RFRA unconstitutional at the state level, the Religious Freedom Restoration Act could have a large role if any of these cases reach the federal level.

It is interesting that the sponsors of the Religious Freedom Restoration Act on both sides of Congress and the President who signed the bill were all Democrats. With the movement of the Democratic Party away from religious norms on issues such as gay marriage and abortion, it is highly doubtful that a bill of this nature would gather such significant Democratic support possibly not even enough to pass if it were introduced today. The polarization that is happening around religious issues will doubtlessly keep the RFRA at the forefront as new questions about acceptable practices are raised. If the Republican Party moves away from the current religious standards in an effort to adapt to reach more of the electorate, which is possible yet unlikely, there could be a movement away from RFRA standards and onto less protective standards.

The Religious Freedom Restoration Act is an important protection for religious freedom. Some say that it might be too restrictive allowing people to claim free exercise burdens just to get out of following the law, but despite this possibility, it is a valuable law that protects people from having their religious beliefs restricted because of a law that might not have meant harm but ended up being applied to their religious   practices.

Conclusion

In summary, religion has been a large part of society for hundreds of years and a large part of American history since the first settlers landed in America. As was seen, the Virginia Statute for Religious Freedom, the First Amendment, and similar pieces of law and literature supporting the free exercise of religion were prominent throughout the early period of the United States. The balance between government interest in regulation and protecting the individual's free exercise of religion was kept fairly well by the Supreme Court for many years. It was not until 1990 in the case *Employment Division v. Smith* that the Court deviated so much from Free Exercise precedents that the US Congress decided it needed to act to make sure that the Court did not swing too far and place too much burden on the individuals whose free exercise of religion were in limbo. Congress passed the Religious Freedom Restoration Act of 1993 in order to codify the Sherbert Test which said that the government cannot burden a person's free exercise of religion even if the law is not written with that intention. The only exemptions are if the government has demonstrated that it has a compelling interest and that the burdening of religion is in the least restrictive means possible. In 1997, the Supreme Court in *City of Boerne v. Flores* declared the RFRA to be unconstitutional as applied to the states, and in 2014, the RFRA became the main defense for Hobby Lobby Stores and other similar corporations who brought a lawsuit against Health and Human Services for burdening their free exercise of religion with the contraception mandate that was implemented as part of the

Religious Freedom in America

Affordable Care Act. This case and others are quite applicable to today's discussion of religion and politics.

Politics and religion are issues that will continue to be prominent in culture whether they are discussed or not. Both of these issues determine where everyone goes in the future. Politics determines the direction the country goes, and religion determines where individuals go after they die. With the polarization surrounding religious issues, the Religious Freedom Restoration Act will continue to be a prominent piece of religious legislation well into the future.

About the Author

Matthew A. Brown is a law student at the University of Akron School of Law. He has a passion for religious liberty and constitutional law. He is also an author, blogger, and baseball enthusiast. His desire is to see the nation strengthened through strong Christian churches, Christian families, and Christian individuals. You can read articles about religion, politics, current events, and more on his blog, amoralandreligiouspeople.wordpress.com. You can also connect with him on Twitter at @MattBrown1575.

Other Books by Matthew A. Brown

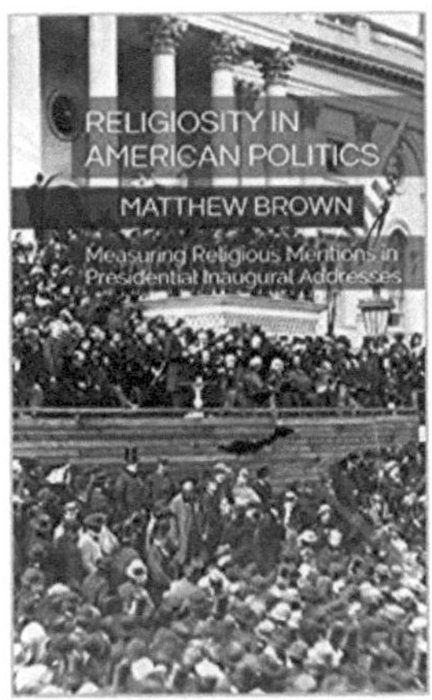

Religiosity in American Politics: Measuring Religious Mentions in Presidential Inaugural Addresses

Religion in American politics is a subject that is almost unconsciously a major part of our political system. Despite the rhetorical "separation of church and state," politicians and citizens both use religion to define and apply their politics. These tendencies raise the questions of which party uses religion more and if the use of religion has increased or decreased over time. This study uses the first fifty-seven Presidential inaugural addresses (Washington-Obama) to determine any trends in the religious mentions of Presidents. The results may surprise you.

Annotated Bibliography

An Act for establishing religious Freedom. 16 January 1786.
Web. 12 November 2014.
<http://www.virginiamemory.com/docs/ReligiousFree.pdf>

The Virginia Statute for Religious Freedom was drafted by
Thomas Jefferson in 1777. It was one of the first times the
freedom of religion was a law. This laid the foundation for the
religion clauses of the First Amendment and later the Religious
Freedom Restoration Act. I will use this source to point out the
religious heritage of our country.

Burwell v. Hobby Lobby Stores, Inc., 573 U.S. ___ (2014). 30
June 2014. Web. 14 November 2014.
<supreme.justia.com/cases/federal/us/573/13-354/>

The *Hobby Lobby* decision was the major Supreme
Court case that raised the question of whether or not the
RFRA applied to for-profit corporations. It was a major blow to
the HHS contraceptive mandate and the Affordable Care Act.
This source gives the background about the decision.

City of Boerne v. Flores 521 U.S. 507 (1997). 25 June 1997.
Web. 13 November 2014.
<supreme.justia.com/cases/federal/us/521/507/case.html>

The *City of Boerne* decision declared that the RFRA was
unconstitutional when applied to the states. The case was
decided three years after the law was signed. It significantly

narrowed the scope of the RFRA. This source will give the reasoning for the decision.

C-SPAN Senate Session. 26 October 1993. Web. 28 October 2014. <http://www.c-span.org/video/?51853-1/senate-session>

The Senate floor debate on the the RFRA was held on October 26, 1993. This source included the video and transcript. This is important because it is the opportunity for the Senators to express their concerns or reasons as to why or why not the bill should be passed. It will give great insight into the thought processes of the Senators.

Employment Division v. Smith. 494 U.S. 872 (1990). n.d. Web. 28 October 2014.
http://www.law.cornell.edu/supremecourt/text/494/872

Employment Division v. Smith was the case that started the discussion for the RFRA. It departed from the Sherbert Test of determining free exercise validity. The Supreme Court decided to not use this test in *Employment Division* which caused the Congress to pass a law codifying the Sherbert Test.

Gonzales v. O Centro Espirita Beneficenteuniao Do Vegetal, 546 U.S. ___ (2006). 21 February 2006. Web. 13 November 2014. <www.law.cornell.edu/supct/html/04-1084.ZO.html>

This is the case that affirmed that the RFRA was constitutional on the federal level.

The Holy Bible: King James Version. New York: Oxford University Press, 1945. Print

This is the King James Version of the Holy Bible. I will use it to refer to the intensity of religious people and their passion for their religion over their government.

Hearing Before the COMMITTEE ON THE JUDICIARY UNITED STATES SENATE One Hundred Second Congress Second Session on S. 2969 A Bill To Protect The Free Exercise Of Religion. 18 September 1992. Web. 10 November 2014. <www.babel.hathitrust.org/cgi/pt?id=pst.000021227936;view=1up;seq=1;skin=mobile>

This was the hearing in the Senate Judiciary Committee on the topic of S. 2969. This will give information about the need for the RFRA and reasons why it should be passed.

H.R.1308 – Religious Freedom Restoration Act of 1993. nd. Web 10 November 2014. www.congress.gov/bill/103rd-congress/house-bill/1308/actions

This is the bill that introduced by Rep. Charles Schumer in the House of Representatives that was eventually signed into law and became the Religious Freedom Restoration Act.

S.2969 – Religious Freedom Restoration Act of 1992. nd. Web.
10 November 2014. <www.congress.gov/bill/102nd-
congress/senate-bill/2969/all-actions>

This is the first bill that was introduced after the case
Employment Division v. Smith by Senator Ted Kennedy in the
102nd Congress. It did not pass, but it did start the
conversation about the need for a Religious Freedom
Restoration Act.

S.578 – Religious Freedom Restoration Act of 1993. nd. Web.
10 November 2014. <www.congress.gov/bill/103rd-
congress/senate-bill/578/all-actions>

Senator Kennedy reintroduced his bill in the 103rd Congress.
H.R. 1308 was passed in lieu of this bill. It kept the discussion
about *Employment Division* and a Religious Freedom
Restoration Act alive.

Virginia Statute for Establishing Religious Freedom (1786). nd.
Web. 12 November 2014.
http://www.encyclopediavirginia.org/Virginia_Statute_for_Est
ablishing_Religious_Freedom_1786

This is another source discussing Jefferson's Virginia Statute
for Religious Freedom. This source gives different insight
about the statute. It will also give background for the RFRA.

Notes

[1] *Virginia Statute for Establishing Religious Freedom (1786).* nd. Web. 12 November 2014. <http://www.encyclopediavirginia.org/Virginia_Statute_for_E stablishing_Religious_Freedom_1786>

[2] *An Act for establishing religious* Freedom. 16 January 1786. Web. 12 November 2014. <http://www.virginiamemory.com/docs/ReligiousFree.pdf>

[3] *Employment Division v. Smith.* 494 U.S. 872 (1990). n.d. Web. 28 October 2014. <http://www.law.cornell.edu/supremecourt/text/494/872>

[4] Ibid.

[5] Ibid.

[6] *Employment Division v. Smith.* 494 U.S. 872 (1990). 28 October 2014. <http://www.law.cornell.edu/supremecourt/text/494/872>

[7] Ibid.

[8] *Employment Division v. Smith.* 494 U.S. 872 (1990). 28 October 2014. <http://www.law.cornell.edu/supremecourt/text/494/872>

[9] Ibid.

[10] Ibid.

[11] *Employment Division v. Smith*. 494 U.S. 872 (1990). 28 October 2014. <http://www.law.cornell.edu/supremecourt/text/494/872>

[12] *S.2969 – Religious Freedom Restoration Act of 1992*. nd. Web. 10 November 2014. <www.congress.gov/bill/102nd-congress/senate-bill/2969/all-actions>

[13] *S.578 – Religious Freedom Restoration Act of 1993*. nd. Web. 10 November 2014. <www.congress.gov/bill/103rd-congress/senate-bill/578/all-actions>

[14] H.R.1308 – Religious Freedom Restoration Act of 1993. nd. Web 10 November 2014. <www.congress.gov/bill/103rd-congress/house-bill/1308/actions>

[15] *Hearing Before the COMMITTEE ON THE JUDICIARY UNITED STATES SENATE One Hundred Second Congress Second Session on S. 2969 A Bill To Protect The Free Exercise Of Religion*. 18 September 1992. Web. 10 November 2014. <www.babel.hathitrust.org/cgi/pt?id=pst.000021227936;view=1up;seq=1;skin=mobile>

[16] Ibid.

[17] *C-SPAN Senate Session*. 26 October 1993. Web. 28 October 2014. <http://www.c-span.org/video/?51853-1/senate-session>

[18] *The Holy Bible: King James Version*. New York: Oxford University Press, 1945. Print

[19] H.R.1308 – Religious Freedom Restoration Act of 1993. nd. Web 10 November 2014. <www.congress.gov/bill/103rd-congress/house-bill/1308/all-actions>

[20] H.R.1308 – Religious Freedom Restoration Act of 1993. nd. Web 10 November 2014. <www.congress.gov/bill/103rd-congress/house-bill/1308>

[21] *City of Boerne v. Flores* 521 U.S. 507 (1997). 25 June 1997. Web. 13 November 2014. <supreme.justia.com/cases/federal/us/521/507/case.html>

[22] *City of Boerne v. Flores* 521 U.S. 507-508 (1997). 25 June 1997. Web. 13 November 2014. <supreme.justia.com/cases/federal/us/521/507/case.html>

[23] Ibid.

[24] Ibid.

[25] *Gonzales v. O Centro Espirita Beneficenteuniao Do Vegetal*, 546 U.S. ___ (2006). 21 February 2006. Web. 13 November 2014. <www.law.cornell.edu/supct/html/04-1084.ZO.html>

[26] *Burwell v. Hobby Lobby Stores, Inc.*, 573 U.S. ___ (2014). 30 June 2014. Web. 14 November 2014. <supreme.justia.com/cases/federal/us/573/13-354/>

[27] Ibid.

[28] *Burwell v. Hobby Lobby Stores, Inc.*, 573 U.S. ___ (2014). 30 June 2014. Web. 14 November 2014. <supreme.justia.com/cases/federal/us/573/13-354/>

[29] Ibid.